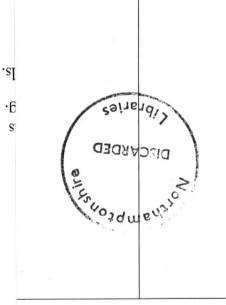

then read to learn!
children learn to read,
can be sure that you're helping

WALLACE, K.   F4

Duckling days

A Note to Parents and Teachers

A Dorling Kindersley Book
www.dk.com

Senior Editor Linda Esposito
Senior Art Editor Andrew Burgess
Managing Art Editor Peter Bailey
Production Josie Alabaster
Photography John Daniels
Reading Consultant
Cliff Moon M.Ed.

Published in Great Britain by
Dorling Kindersley Limited
9 Henrietta Street
London WC2E 8PS

2 4 6 8 10 9 7 5 3

A CIP catalogue record for this book is
available from the British Library.
ISBN 0-7513-5897-5

Colour reproduction by Colourscan, Singapore
Printed and bound in Belgium by Proost

The publisher would like to thank the following
for their kind permission to reproduce their
photographs:
a=above; c=centre; b=below/bottom; l=left;
r=right; t=top

Barrie Watts: 5cr, 6b, 7tr, 26cl (below), 26cr (below),
27t, 28cl (above)

EYEWITNESS  READERS

BEGINNING 1 TO READ

Duckling Days

Written by Karen Wallace

DK

DORLING KINDERSLEY
London • New York • Moscow • Sydney

In the grass
beside the river
a mother duck
builds her nest.

She gathers grass and
makes a hollow.

She lines her nest with
downy feathers.

nest

In a nest
beside the river
a mother duck
lays six white eggs.

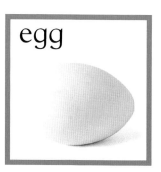

egg

She keeps them warm
beneath her body.
Inside each egg
a duckling grows.

A duckling hatches
from his egg.

shell He cracks the shell.

He makes a hole
with his tiny beak.

He taps and pushes.

He breaks out of the shell
and squeezes out.

Other ducklings
hatch beside him.
At first their legs
are weak and wobbly.

Their downy feathers
are wet and sticky but
they dry out quickly
beside their mother.

Mother duck has
six fluffy ducklings.
She leads them down
towards the river.

But one little duckling
is left behind.

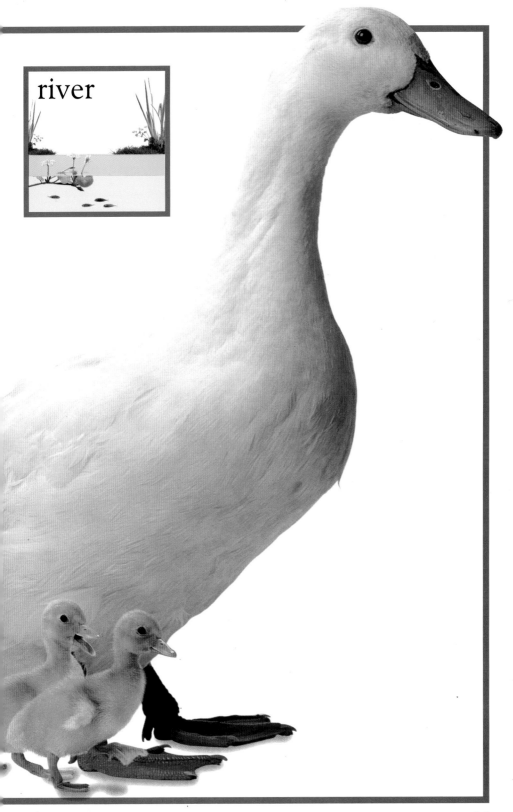

river

13

cheep
cheep

One little duckling
cheeps and twitters.
Where is his mother?

Where can
she be?

The little duckling
runs to find her.

cheep

He's frightened of being
on his own.

Five ducklings jump
into the water.
They push and paddle
with their webbed feet.

webbed
feet

cheep

One little duckling
finds his family.

Mother duck checks
her ducklings.

Six fluffy babies
swim beside her.

In the river
the water is deep.
Mother duck dives
and leaves her ducklings.

She nibbles plants.
She chases beetles.

Six little ducklings
look around them.

Where is mother duck?
Where can she be?

cheep

cheep

cheep

Cheep! Cheep!
The ducklings call for mother.

cheep

cheep

cheep

A bee buzzes in the air.

A frog croaks from a lily pad.

croak

Two birds sing on a branch.

tweet tweet

But mother duck
does not answer.
Where has she gone?
Where can she be?

Quack! Quack!
She pops up in the water!

quack

quack

cheep

cheep

cheep

Cheep! Cheep!
Her ducklings huddle round her.

Next time
they will be much braver!

cheep

cheep

cheep

The growing ducklings
snap at tadpoles.
They pull at pondweed
with their yellow bills.

bill

They like to dabble
in the water.

They watch their mother.
They do what she does.

The ducklings' down
grows into feathers.

feathers

They watch
their mother clean
her feathers.

She flaps and fluffs.

She plucks
and preens.

She strokes
and smooths.

Mother duck
is combed
and clean!

Five young ducks waddle
from the river.

They shake the water
from their backs.
They flap their wings
just like their mother.
They clean their feathers
with their beaks.

wing

One young duck
dabbles in the water.
He's happy being
on his own.

Picture Word List

nest

page 5

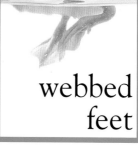
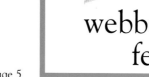
webbed feet
page 16

egg

page 6

bill

page 26

shell
page 8

feathers
page 28

river

page 13

wing
page 30